365 DAYS OF
DAD
JOKES

AWFULLY GOOD GAGS...

ALL YEAR ROUND

JIM CHUMLEY

Published in the United States by Viva Editions, an imprint of Start Midnight, LLC, 221 River Street, Ninth Floor, Hoboken, New Jersey 07030.

Printed in the United States

10 9 8 7 6 5 4 3 2 1

Trade paper ISBN: 978-1-63228-090-9

E-book ISBN: 978-1-63228-147-0

INTRODUCTION

Ever heard a joke that was so bad, it was good? It's more than likely that the person making you groan, while also trying not to laugh, was your dad—or someone else's dad!

There's something very special about dad jokes: they are always terrible, sometimes funny and occasionally hilarious. So, whether you're a dad looking to add to your collection of brain-bustingly awful gags, or you'd like to beat your old man at his own game, this is the book for you.

TO..

FROM..

Armed with enough witty one-liners, ridiculous observations, groansome puns and classic jokes to last an entire year, you'll be able to make your audience burst out laughing while shaking their heads and pleading with you to shut up.

But if you're a dad, don't you dare stop cracking those funnies! You've earned your right to tell a dad joke!

And if you're not a dad . . . well, there's nothing to stop you getting in on the act of cringeworthy comedy.

So, what are you waiting for? Get reading and start seeking out your reluctant audience now!

JANUARY

Why do dads feel the need to tell such bad jokes? **They just want to help you become a groan up.**

I've been thinking about taking up meditation. I figure it's better than sitting around doing nothing.

3

What kind of car does a sheep
like to drive?
A Lamborghini.

4

What did the drummer call his
twin daughters?
Anna One, Anna Two!

(5)

What do you call a belt made
of watches?
A waist of time.

(6)

What's an astronaut's favorite
part of a computer?
The space bar.

(7)

I could tell a joke about pizza,
but it's a little cheesy.

(8)

I TOLD MY DOCTOR I HEARD BUZZING, BUT HE SAID IT'S JUST A BUG GOING AROUND.

Why are elevator jokes so funny?

Because they work on many levels.

WHY ARE DOORS A BIG HIT ON SOCIAL MEDIA?
EVERYONE LOOKS FOR THEIR HANDLES.

WHICH VEGETABLE IS KIND TO EVERYONE?
THE SWEET POTATO.

6:30 IS MY FAVORITE TIME OF THE DAY, HANDS DOWN.

13

My wife is mad at me because she asked me to sync her phone, so I threw it in the sea.

14

Whenever I go to the park with my dog, the ducks are always trying to bite him. Serves me right for buying a pure bread dog.

(15)

What happened when the world's tongue-twister champion got arrested? **They gave him a tough sentence.**

(16)

I have a spooky joke about mathematics, but I'm 2^2 to say it.

MOST PEOPLE CAN'T TELL THE DIFFERENCE BETWEEN ENTOMOLOGY AND ETYMOLOGY. I CAN'T FIND THE WORDS FOR HOW MUCH THIS BUGS ME.

How do you row a canoe filled with puppies?
Use a doggy paddle.

(19)

TWO GOLDFISH ARE IN A TANK. ONE SAYS TO THE OTHER, "DO YOU KNOW HOW TO DRIVE THIS THING?"

(20)

Want to hear a joke about paper?
Nevermind – it's tearable.

What do you call it when a group
of apes starts a company?
Monkey business.

Why did the man fall down the well?
**Because he couldn't see
that well.**

23

What's E.T. short for?
Because he's only got tiny legs!

(24)

My boss told me to have a good
day, so I went home.

(25)

My wife asked me to go get 6
cans of Sprite from the store.
I realized when I got home
that I had picked 7 Up.

WHAT WOULD THE TERMINATOR BE CALLED IN HIS RETIREMENT?

THE EXTERMINATOR.

SUNDAYS ARE ALWAYS A LITTLE SAD, BUT THE DAY BEFORE IS A SADDER DAY.

28

I USED TO HATE FACIAL HAIR, BUT THEN IT GREW ON ME.

What did the accountant say while auditing a document?

"This is taxing."

Why do you never see
elephants hiding in trees?
Because they're so good at it.

Dogs can't operate MRI
machines. But catscan.

FEBRUARY

I lost my job at the bank on my first day. A woman asked me to check her balance, so I pushed her over.

How does a salad say grace?
Lettuce pray.

(3)

WHICH COUNTRY'S CAPITAL IS GROWING THE FASTEST?

IRELAND. EVERY DAY IT'S DUBLIN.

(4)

DID YOU HEAR ABOUT THE KIDNAPPING AT SCHOOL?

IT TURNED OUT OK – HE WOKE UP.

(5)

A cheeseburger walks into a bar.
The bartender says, "Sorry, we
don't serve food here."

(6)

Which invention allows us to
see through walls?
Windows.

7

Did you hear about the guy who
invented the knock-knock joke?
He won the "no-bell" prize.

8

What do you call a fibbing cat?
A lion.

My wife and I let astrology get
between us. It just Taurus apart.

**DO MASCARA AND LIPSTICK
EVER ARGUE?**

SURE, BUT THEN THEY MAKE-UP.

**WHERE DO WASPS LIKE TO
EAT LUNCH?**

A BEE-STRO.

(12)

What part of the playground
is always exhausted?
The tire swing.

(13)

I know a bunch of good jokes
about umbrellas, but they
usually go over people's heads.

It takes guts to be an
organ donor.

What do you call a fake noodle?
An impasta.

(16)

I'm so good at sleeping, I can do
it with my eyes closed!

17

I ORDERED A CHICKEN AND AN EGG ONLINE. I'LL LET YOU KNOW.

What is the most popular
fish in the sea?
A starfish.

5/4 OF PEOPLE ADMIT THEY'RE BAD AT FRACTIONS.

When I was a kid, my dad got fired from his job as a road worker for theft. I refused to believe he would steal anything, but when I got home, the signs were all there.

(21)

If the early bird gets the worm,
I'll sleep in until there's a
bacon sandwich.

(22)

Did you hear about the
surgeon who performed quick
surgeries on insects?
He did one on the fly.

(23)

Why do some couples go
to the gym?

**Because they want their
relationship to work out.**

Two dads walked into a bar.
The third dad ducked.

WHY DIDN'T HAN SOLO ENJOY
HIS STEAK DINNER?

IT WAS CHEWIE.

WHAT DO YOU CALL A
PUDGY PSYCHIC?

A FOUR-CHIN TELLER.

HOW DO CELEBRITIES STAY COOL?

THEY HAVE MANY FANS.

(28)

MY WIFE ASKED ME TO STOP SINGING "WONDERWALL" TO HER. I SAID, "MAYBE . . ."

What do you call a toothless bear?

A gummy bear!

MARCH

1

I only know 25 letters of the alphabet. I don't know "Y."

2

Why do seagulls fly over the sea?

Because if they flew over the bay, we'd call them bagels.

3

How does the moon cut his hair?
Eclipse it.

4

What did the zero say to
the eight?
That belt looks good on you.

5

Why don't pirates take a bath
before they walk the plank?
They just wash up on shore.

6

Have you heard about the
chocolate guitar?
It sounds pretty sweet.

7

If you're American when you go
into a bathroom and American
when you come out, what are you
while you're in the bathroom?
European.

KID: DAD, DID YOU GET A HAIRCUT?
DAD: NO, I GOT THEM ALL CUT!

DID YOU HEAR THE RUMOR
ABOUT BUTTER?
WELL, I'M NOT GOING TO SPREAD IT!

WHAT DID ONE HAT SAY TO
THE OTHER?
"STAY HERE! I'M GOING ON AHEAD."

11

Singing in the shower is fun
until you get soap in your
mouth. Then it's a soap opera.

12

If a child refuses to sleep
during nap time, are they guilty
of resisting a rest?

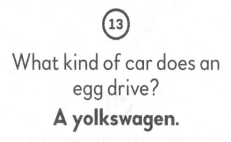

What kind of car does an
egg drive?
A yolkswagen.

I used to play piano by ear.
Now I use my hands.

What do you call two
octopuses that look the same?
Itentacle.

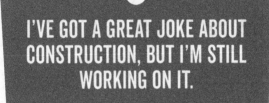

16

I'VE GOT A GREAT JOKE ABOUT CONSTRUCTION, BUT I'M STILL WORKING ON IT.

17

What does a house wear?
Address.

(18)

I ONCE GOT FIRED FROM A CANNED JUICE COMPANY. I JUST COULDN'T CONCENTRATE.

What's a vampire's favorite type of ship?
A blood vessel.

What does a bee use to
brush its hair?

A honeycomb.

Why wouldn't the skeleton
climb the mountain?

It didn't have the guts to.

What do you call cheese
that isn't yours?
Nacho cheese.

What kind of shoes do
ninjas wear?
Sneakers.

I have a joke about a broken
pencil, but it's pointless.

WHAT KIND OF DRINK CAN BE BITTER AND SWEET?

REALI-TEA.

HOW DO YOU WEIGH A MILLENNIAL?

IN INSTAGRAMS.

WHAT DID THE DISHWASHER SAY TO THE OVEN AFTER A PRODUCTIVE DAY?

YOU'VE BEEN ON FIRE TODAY!

(28)

SOME PEOPLE PICK THEIR NOSE, BUT I WAS JUST BORN WITH MINE.

(29)

What do you call an elephant that doesn't matter?

Irrelephant.

I'm reading a book about anti-gravity. It's impossible to put down.

We all know about Murphy's Law: Anything that can go wrong will go wrong. But have you heard of Cole's Law? It's thinly sliced cabbage.

APRIL

How did the dad prank his daughter using fake dog dirt on April Fools' Day?

He told her to look out for her new sham-poo in the shower.

I decided to sell my vacuum cleaner – it was just gathering dust.

HOW DO YOU CURE A FEAR OF A SPEED BUMP?

YOU SLOWLY GET OVER IT.

④

I KNOW A LOT OF JOKES ABOUT RETIRED PEOPLE, BUT NONE OF THEM WORK.

WHAT'S THE BEST-SMELLING INSECT?

A DEODOR-ANT.

(6)

My friend was at the Apple
Store and saw a crime being
committed. Guess that makes
him an iWitness.

(7)

What happens when a
strawberry gets run over while
crossing the street?
A traffic jam.

What's a robot's
favorite snack?
Computer chips.

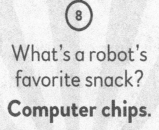

Why is Peter Pan
always flying?
Because he neverlands.

Mountains aren't just funny.
They're hill areas.

WHAT'S THE BEST WAY TO WATCH
A FISHING TOURNAMENT?

ON A LIVE STREAM.

DON'T TRUST ATOMS. THEY
MAKE UP EVERYTHING!

THE PAST, THE PRESENT AND
THE FUTURE WALKED INTO A BAR.
IT WAS TENSE.

What did one plate say to
another plate?

Tonight, dinner's on me.

Why do pancakes always
win at baseball?

They have the best batter.

Did you hear about the racing
snail who got rid of his shell?
It made him sluggish.

What kind of shape gets
knighted?
Cir-cles.

Which animals are the best to
call if you get locked out
of your house?
Monkeys.

(19)

TIME FLIES LIKE AN ARROW. FRUIT FLIES LIKE A BANANA.

(20)

What's a chiropractor's
favorite type of music?

Hip pop.

What do you call a boomerang
that doesn't come back?
A stick.

Why did the computer get mad
at the printer?
**Because it didn't like its
toner voice.**

What happened to the illegally
parked frog?
It got toad.

Did you hear about the king
who was exactly 12 inches tall?
He was a great ruler!

I have a joke about chemistry,
but I don't think it'll get a
reaction.

(26)

To the person who stole my
place in the queue: I'm after
you now.

Kid: I'll call you later.
Dad: No, call me Dad.

What did the right eye say
to the left eye?

**Between you and me,
something smells.**

WHAT DID THE DAD SAY AS HE REVERSED THE CAR?

AH, THIS TAKES ME BACK.

I JUST GOT A PROMOTION AT THE FARM. NOW I'M THE C-I-E-I-O.

MAY

I used to be addicted to the Hokey Pokey, but then I turned myself around.

What do you call a cow during an earthquake?
A milkshake.

③

What do you call a man with
a rubber toe?

Roberto.

④

What did Obi-Wan say to Luke
when he was having trouble
using chopsticks?

"Use the fork, Luke."

How do you make
Lady Gaga mad?
Poke her face.

6

Why can't a leopard hide?
**Because it'll always
be spotted.**

7

To the person who stole my
energy drinks: I bet you can't
sleep at night.

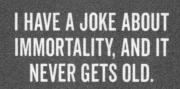

8

I HAVE A JOKE ABOUT IMMORTALITY, AND IT NEVER GETS OLD.

9

What do you call an unpredictable camera?

A loose Canon.

I like telling my kid jokes.
Sometimes he laughs!

Why can't you hear a
psychiatrist using the toilet?
Because the "P" is silent.

I've been bored recently, so
I decided to take up fencing.
The neighbors keep demanding
that I put it back.

What did the police officer say
to his belly button?
You're under a vest.

Did you know corduroy
pillows are in style? They're
making headlines.

What time did the man go
to the dentist?
Tooth hurt-y.

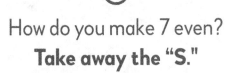

How do you make 7 even?
Take away the "S."

What does a lemon say when it
answers the phone?
Yellow!

HOW DOES A PENGUIN BUILD ITS HOUSE?

IGLOOS IT TOGETHER.

HOW MANY TICKLES DOES IT TAKE TO MAKE AN OCTOPUS LAUGH?

TEN TICKLES.

KID: DAD, CAN YOU PUT MY SHOES ON?

DAD: NO, I DON'T THINK THEY'LL FIT ME.

(21)

TWO PEANUTS WERE WALKING DOWN THE STREET. ONE WAS ASSAULTED.

(22)

What did the dad say as he held his stepladder?

I never knew my real ladder.

What did the dad buffalo say
when he left for work?
Bison.

24

To the person who stole
my laptop with my copy of
Microsoft Office on it: I will
find you. You have my Word!

25

What did the two pieces of bread
say on their wedding day?
It was loaf at first sight.

26

I have a joke about
procrastination, but I'll tell
it to you later.

What do you call a hippie's wife?
Mississippi.

Why can't you send a duck to
outer space?
**Because the bill would be
astronomical.**

(29)

Can anyone tell me what
oblivious means, because I
have no idea.

WHAT DO YOU CALL A DEER WITH NO EYES?

NO-EYE DEER.

WHAT DO YOU CALL A DEER WITH NO EYES AND NO LEGS?

STILL NO-EYE DEER.

JUNE

(1)

I can tolerate algebra, maybe even a little calculus, but geometry is where I draw the line.

(2)

My boss asked me why I only get sick on work days. I said it must be my weekend immune system.

What do you call a fish
with no eye?
A fsh.

(4)

Why are balloons so
expensive?
Due to inflation.

MY WIFE ASKED ME TO PUT
KETCHUP ON THE SHOPPING
LIST. NOW I CAN'T READ IT.

What do you call a fish
wearing a bowtie?
Sofishticated.

(7)

I had a dream that I weighed less than a thousandth of a gram. I was like, 0mg!

(8)

What did the baker say when she won an award?

"It was a piece of cake."

(9)

Why was the cow such a heartthrob on the farm?

He was a s-moo-th talker.

(10)

I won't buy anything with
Velcro. It's a total rip-off.

(11)

Where did the mathematician
visit on his trip to New York?
Times Square.

What do you call two
monkeys that share an
Amazon account?
Prime mates.

Where do young trees go
to learn?
Elementree school.

Can February March?
No, but April May!

WHAT DOES GARLIC DO WHEN IT GETS HOT?

IT TAKES ITS CLOVES OFF.

HOW DO LAWYERS SAY GOODBYE?

SUE YOU LATER!

17

DID YOU HEAR ABOUT THE CIRCUS FIRE?

IT WAS IN TENTS.

(18)

WHAT DO CLOUDS PUT ON IN THE MORNING?
THUNDERWEAR.

(19)

What kind of bird is always getting hurt?
The owl.

(20)

Why was the ghost so tired?
He worked the graveyard shift.

(21)

Why couldn't the couple get
married at the library?
Because it was all booked up.

Why did the cashier rip money
in half?

**He'd been asked to break a
twenty-dollar bill.**

What's it called when kittens
get stuck in a tree?

A cat-astrophe.

Every night, I have a hard time
remembering something, but
then it dawns on me.

25

I was wondering why the frisbee
kept getting bigger and bigger.
Then it hit me.

26

Which side of a tree grows
the most branches?
The outside.

DID YOU HEAR ABOUT THE SQUARE
THAT GOT INTO A CAR ACCIDENT?

NOW IT'S A RECT-ANGLE!

WHAT BREED OF DOG CAN JUMP
HIGHER THAN A HOUSE?

ALL OF THEM — HOUSES
CAN'T JUMP.

29

The guy that invented the umbrella was going to call it the brella. But he hesitated.

30

I can kayak. Canoe?

JULY

①

Why can't you ever run through a campsite?

You can only ran – it's always past tents.

②

I don't trust trees. They seem kind of shady.

WHAT DO YOU CALL A FRENCHMAN WEARING SANDALS?

PHILLIPE FLOP.

WHICH U.S. STATE HAS THE MOST STREETS?

RHODE ISLAND.

3(5)

I WENT TO THE ZOO AND SAW A BAGUETTE IN A CAGE. THE ZOOKEEPER SAID IT WAS BREAD IN CAPTIVITY.

6

Why did the cookie cry?
**Because his dad was a wafer
so long.**

7

What do Kermit the Frog and
Attila the Hun have in common?
**They share the same
middle name.**

8

How do billboards
communicate?
By using sign language.

9

AFTER DINNER, MY WIFE ASKED
IF I COULD CLEAR THE TABLE. I
NEEDED A RUNNING START,
BUT I MADE IT!

10

Why can't you give Elsa
a balloon?

Because she will let it go.

11

Did you hear about the two
dads who stole a calendar?
They each got six months.

12

How do you get a baby to sleep
in outer space?
Rocket.

13

When does an ocean not
have water?
When it's on a map.

(14)

When should you go at red
and stop at green?

When eating a watermelon.

(15)

Why don't trees take the bus?

**They can never decide on
the best root.**

(16)

How do you organize a
party on Mars?

Planet.

(17)

What kind of shoes does a
lazy person wear?
Loafers.

(18)

Why do nurses like red crayons?
**Sometimes they have to
draw blood.**

WHAT DID TENNESSEE?
THE SAME THING AS ARKANSAS.

WHY DO MELONS HAVE WEDDINGS?
BECAUSE THEY CANTALOUPE.

WHICH BEAR IS THE MOST
CONDESCENDING?
A PAN-DUH!

22

I USED TO BE ADDICTED TO SOAP,
BUT I'M CLEAN NOW.

23

What's the most detail-
oriented ocean?
The Pacific.

(24)

Swimming with sharks is so expensive – it cost me an arm and a leg.

(25)

Today, my son asked, "Can I have a bookmark?" I burst into tears. He's 11 and he still doesn't know my name is Brian.

What do you call a factory that makes adequate products?
A satisfactory.

My fingers are reliable. I can count on all of them.

What did the caretaker say when he jumped out of the cupboard?
Supplies!

What did one wall say to
the other?

"I'll meet you at the corner."

I asked my dog what's two
minus two. He said nothing.

What did the baby corn say to
the mama corn?

"Where's pop corn?"

AUGUST

①

What did the dad say when
his golden retriever was caught
eating a hot dog?
It's a dog eat dog world out there.

What's Forrest Gump's
online password?
1forrest1

③

My wife said I should do lunges
to stay in shape. That would be
a big step forward.

④

Have you heard about the
restaurant on the moon?
**Great food, but no
atmosphere.**

⑤

How do you get a squirrel
to like you?
Act like a nut.

(6)

What do a tick and the Eiffel
Tower have in common?
They're both Paris sites.

(7)

Where do boats go when
they're sick?
To the doc.

(8)

Why did the dad get fired from
the banana factory?
**He kept throwing away the
bent ones.**

WHAT TYPE OF BUILDING HAS THE MOST STORIES?

A LIBRARY.

WHY DON'T EGGS TELL JOKES?

THEY'D CRACK EACH OTHER UP.

WHAT DID THE SEA SAY TO THE BEACH?

NOTHING, IT JUST WAVED.

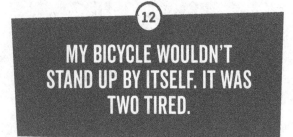

(12)

MY BICYCLE WOULDN'T STAND UP BY ITSELF. IT WAS TWO TIRED.

(13)

Why did Mickey Mouse take a trip into outer space?

He wanted to find Pluto.

(14)

What do you call a pig that
does karate?
A pork chop.

(15)

Dear Mathematics, grow up
and solve your own problems.

What did the slow tomato
say to its friends?
"Don't worry, I'll ketchup."

Did you hear about the jaguar
that ate a tightrope walker?

**It was craving a
well-balanced meal.**

(18)

My wife complained that I have
no sense of direction.

**So, I packed up my stuff
and right!**

(19)

What do you call a pony with
a sore throat?
A little hoarse.

(20)

Why are skeletons so calm?
**Nothing gets under
their skin.**

(21)

Why was Cinderella kicked off
the football team?
She ran away from the ball.

WHY DON'T CRABS GIVE TO CHARITY?

BECAUSE THEY'RE SHELL-FISH.

WHAT DO YOU CALL A BLIND DINOSAUR?

DOYOUTHINKHESAURUS?

24

What do you call a man with
just a nose and no body?
No body nose.

25

To the person who stole my
bed: I won't rest until I find you.

26

What did the pirate say on his
eightieth birthday?
"Aye Matey!"

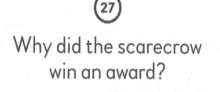

Why did the scarecrow
win an award?
He was out standing in his field.

Where do sharks go on vacation?
Finland.

Where do you learn to make
a banana split?
Sundae school.

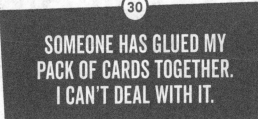

(30)

SOMEONE HAS GLUED MY
PACK OF CARDS TOGETHER.
I CAN'T DEAL WITH IT.

(31)

What is a knight's favorite fish?
A swordfish.

SEPTEMBER

1

I don't enjoy playing football,
I'm just doing it for kicks.

2

What do you call a sleeping bull?
A bulldozer.

Wait, you don't want to hear a
joke about potassium? K.

Why can't a nose be
12 inches long?
Because then it would be a foot.

I have a joke about being an
electrician, but it's too shocking.

(6)

Kid: Dad, can you put the cat out?

Dad: I didn't know it was on fire.

(7)

My dad told me a terrible joke about boxing. I guess I missed the punchline.

Have you ever tried to catch
fog? I tried yesterday but I mist.

9

If money doesn't grow on
trees, then why do banks
have branches?

What do lions use to look at
their manes?
Mirroars.

WHY DO TALL PEOPLE GET ALONG SO WELL?

BECAUSE THEY SEE EYE TO EYE.

WHY ARE SPIDERS SO GOOD AT RESEARCH?

THEY CAN FIND EVERYTHING ON THE WEB.

I USED TO BE A FITNESS COACH. THEN I GAVE MY TOO-WEAK NOTICE.

(14)

Did I tell you the time I fell in
love while doing a backflip?
I was heels over head!

(15)

Why was the fridge dripping?
It was full of leeks.

Justice is a dish best served cold. If it were served warm, it would be justwater.

I used to eat a watch for lunch, but it was too time-consuming.

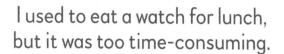

How can you tell if a tree is a dogwood tree?
By its bark.

MY WIFE TEXTED ME FROM THE STORE TO SAY THEY'RE OUT OF PASTA, AND WE'RE PENNELESS.

20

How can you tell if a swimming pool is safe to dive into?

It deep ends.

21

Which bathroom appliance would
be the worst life preserver?
The sink.

22

Why is sand so optimistic?
It has a can-dune attitude.

23

What part of the museum makes
everyone sneeze?
The sta-tues.

(24)

We're renovating the house. The first floor is going great, but the second floor is another story.

(25)

Why did the envelope take so long to get ready?
It had to get addressed.

(26)

The bank keeps calling me to give me compliments. They say I have an "outstanding balance."

(27)

I had a happy childhood.
My dad used to put me in tires
and roll me down hills. Those
were Goodyears.

(28)

I tried to run a dating service
for chickens, but I was
struggling to make hens meet.

**WHAT DID THE GEOMETRY TEACHER
SAY WHEN THE CLASS HAD
TROUBLE SOLVING A PROBLEM?**

"LET'S TRY A DIFFERENT ANGLE."

**DID YOU HEAR ABOUT THE
HANDSOME SPRINTER?**

HE WAS REALLY DASHING.

OCTOBER

When it's raining cats and dogs, be careful not to step in a poodle.

My therapist told me I have problems expressing my emotions. Can't say I'm surprised.

(3)

A skeleton walks into a bar and says, "Hey, bartender. I'll have one beer and a mop."

(4)

I want to name my puppies Rolex and Timex so I can have watch dogs.

(5)

At first, I thought my chiropractor wasn't any good, but now I stand corrected.

(6)

How does Darth Vader like
his toast?
On the dark side.

(7)

What's red and smells like
blue paint?
Red paint.

A MAGICIAN WAS WALKING DOWN THE STREET, THEN TURNED INTO A STORE.

9

What do you call a burger on wheels?
Fast food!

10

What did the fish say when
it hit a wall?
"Dam."

11

When does a joke become
a dad joke?
When it becomes apparent.

12

What's the difference between a
badly dressed kid on a bicycle and
a well-dressed kid on a tricycle?
Attire.

(13)

What did the dryer say to the
boring duvet cover that just got
out of the washing machine?
"Don't be such a wet blanket."

(14)

Whenever I try to eat
healthily, a chocolate bar looks
at me and Snickers.

(15)

Barbers... you have to take
your hat off to them.

(16)

I was going to tell a
time-traveling joke, but
you guys didn't like it.

IF TWO VEGANS GET INTO AN ARGUMENT, IS IT STILL CALLED A BEEF?

DID YOU HEAR ABOUT THE OVERCROWDED GRAVEYARD? PEOPLE WERE DYING TO GET IN.

WHAT DO YOU CALL A FLY WITHOUT WINGS?

A WALK.

(20)

WHY WAS 6 AFRAID OF 7? BECAUSE 7 ATE 9.

What does a clock do when it's hungry?
It goes back 4 seconds.

22

I want a job cleaning mirrors.
It's something I can really see
myself doing.

23

What grades did the pirate
get in her exams?
Seven Cs.

24

What's the difference between
an alligator and a crocodile?
**One you'll see later; the other
you'll see in a while.**

(25)

Why did the toilet paper
roll downhill?

To get to the bottom.

(26)

What has one head, one foot
and four legs?

A bed.

27

What did the animals tell Simba
when he walked too slowly?

"Mufasa!"

28

What do you call someone who
points out the obvious?

**Someone who points out
the obvious.**

29

How do snails fight?

They slug it out.

WHAT KIND OF NOISE DOES A WITCH'S CAR MAKE?

BRRRROOOOM, BRRROOOOM.

WHAT DO YOU CALL A NAUGHTY LAMB DRESSED UP LIKE A SKELETON FOR HALLOWEEN?

BAAAD TO THE BONE.

NOVEMBER

Did you hear about the mobile phones' wedding?
The ceremony was OK, but the reception was terrific.

Sore throats are a pain in the neck.

③

How do you make holy water?
You boil the hell out of it.

④

It was called the Dark Ages
because there were far too
many knights.

⑤

What's the loudest kind of pet?
A trumpet.

(6)

DOES ANYONE NEED AN ARK? BECAUSE I NOAH GUY.

Why can't you play games
in the jungle?

**Because there are too
many cheetahs.**

What do you get when you combine a rhetorical question and a joke?

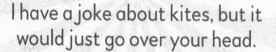

I have a joke about kites, but it would just go over your head.

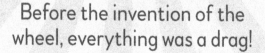

Before the invention of the wheel, everything was a drag!

(11)

What did Winnie the Pooh say
to his agent?

"Show me the honey!"

(12)

I just wrote a book on reverse
psychology. Do not read it.

My favorite word is "drool."
It just rolls off the tongue.

Why don't ants get sick?
They have anty-bodies.

(15)

A communist joke isn't funny
unless *everyone* gets it.

WHAT'S GREEN, FUZZY AND WOULD HURT
IF IT FELL ON YOU OUT OF A TREE?

A POOL TABLE.

HOW DO YOU GET A GOOD PRICE ON A
SLED? YOU HAVE TOBOGGAN.

I HAD A NECK BRACE FITTED YEARS AGO
AND I'VE NEVER LOOKED BACK SINCE.

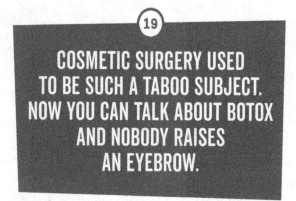

19

COSMETIC SURGERY USED
TO BE SUCH A TABOO SUBJECT.
NOW YOU CAN TALK ABOUT BOTOX
AND NOBODY RAISES
AN EYEBROW.

20

Why are social media influencers
afraid to go out at night?

They're always being followed.

How does a rabbi make his coffee?
He-brews it.

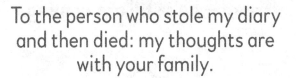

To the person who stole my diary
and then died: my thoughts are
with your family.

What do sprinters eat
before a race?
Nothing – they fast.

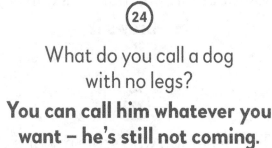

24

What do you call a dog
with no legs?
**You can call him whatever you
want – he's still not coming.**

25

A guy walks into a bar . . .
and gets disqualified from the
limbo contest.

I spent a lot of time, money and effort childproofing my house . . . but the kids still get in.

What do you do when you see a spaceman?
Park in it man.

I'm starting a new dating service in Prague. It's called Czech-Mate.

LAST NIGHT MY WIFE AND I
WATCHED TWO FILMS BACK-TO-
BACK. LUCKILY I WAS THE ONE
FACING THE TV.

TWO CANNIBALS ARE EATING A
CLOWN. ONE SAYS TO THE OTHER,
"DOES THIS TASTE FUNNY TO YOU?"

DECEMBER

What did one snowman say
to the other?
"Can you smell carrots?"

If athletes get athlete's foot,
what do elves get?
Mistletoes.

3

England doesn't have a
kidney bank. But it does have
a Liverpool.

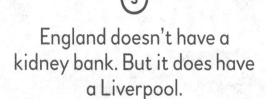

4

Do you know the story about the
chicken that crossed the road?
Me neither, I couldn't follow it.

5

I don't trust stairs. They're
always up to something.

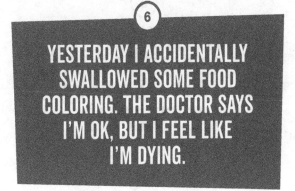

6

YESTERDAY I ACCIDENTALLY
SWALLOWED SOME FOOD
COLORING. THE DOCTOR SAYS
I'M OK, BUT I FEEL LIKE
I'M DYING.

7

Why do golfers always pack an
extra pair of socks?
In case they get a hole in one.

(8)

I SLEPT LIKE A LOG LAST NIGHT. I WOKE UP IN THE FIREPLACE.

Did you hear about the dad who quit his job at the doughnut factory?

He was fed up with the hole business.

What do you get when you cross a
snowman and a vampire?
Frostbite.

What do you call a group of killer
whales playing instruments?
An Orca-stra.

What is the difference between
an angry circus owner and a
Roman barber?
**One is a raving showman, while
the other is a shaving Roman.**

An invisible man married an invisible woman. The kids were nothing to look at.

I remember the first time I saw a remote control. I thought to myself, "Well, this changes everything."

I gave away all my used batteries today, free of charge.

WHY DID THE POWERPOINT PRESENTATION CROSS THE ROAD?
TO GET TO THE OTHER SLIDE.

WHY SHOULD YOU NEVER USE "BEEF STEW" AS A PASSWORD?
IT'S NOT STROGANOFF.

WHAT DID MARS ASK SATURN?
"HEY, CAN YOU GIVE ME A RING SOMETIME?"

(19)

IT'S INAPPROPRIATE TO MAKE A "DAD JOKE" IF YOU'RE NOT A DAD. IT'S A FAUX PA.

(20)

What do you get if you cross an angry sheep with a moody cow?

An animal that's in a baaaaaaaaad moooooooood.

Why did the mushroom get invited
to the Christmas party?
Because he was a fungi.

Did you know that milk is the
fastest liquid on earth?
**It's pasteurized before you
even see it.**

How did Ebenezer Scrooge score a
goal at the football match?
The ghost of Christmas passed!

How much does it cost Santa Claus to park his sleigh?
Nothing – it's on the house.

How did Darth Vader know what Luke Skywalker got him for Christmas?
He felt his presents.

What do you call it when a snowman throws a tantrum?
A meltdown.

I'M ON A SEAFOOD DIET.
I SEE FOOD AND I EAT IT.

What has more letters than
the alphabet?
The post office.

KID: WHAT'S THE BEST THING
ABOUT SWITZERLAND?

DAD: I DON'T KNOW, BUT THE FLAG
IS A BIG PLUS.

I'M AFRAID FOR THE CALENDAR.
ITS DAYS ARE NUMBERED.

What's the difference between
a dad joke and a bad joke?
The first letter.